To:

From:

D1611788

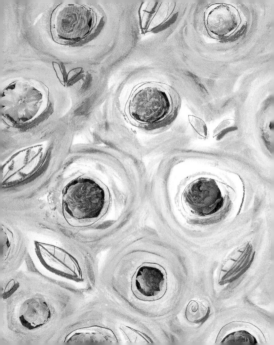

The Little Book of

Spells

By Suzanne Siegel Zenkel

Illustrated by Julia Binfield

Peter Pauper Press, Inc.
White Plains, New York

For Dad, with love

Illustrations copyright © 2002
Julia Binfield/Lilla Rogers Studio

Designed by Heather Zschock

Text copyright © 2002
Peter Pauper Press, Inc.
202 Mamaroneck Avenue
White Plains, NY 10601
All rights reserved
ISBN 0-88088-879-2
Printed in China
7 6 5 4 3 2

Visit us at www.peterpauper.com

THE LITTLE BOOK OF

Spells

love luck
new >>>>
beginnings

CONTENTS

INTRODUCTION

For centuries, people have looked to spellcraft to enhance their lives and environment. Everyone has the power to cast spells. All you need are positive intent, concentrated focus, and the ability to channel your energy.

Spellwork is both super and natural. It is a way of harnessing, building, and directing energy, to bring about positive changes in our lives. Spellcraft derives its momentum from natural phenomena such as Earth, Air, Water, and Fire.

Does what you wish for seem unattainable? Spellcraft can help you recognize opportunities you didn't know existed. It can lead to a life of personal growth and spiritual fulfillment.

The spells that follow employ scents, stones, candles, herbs, and other things readily available. Spellcasting does not require money or space, but rather a sincere faith in yourself and the assurance that you can achieve your desired goal. With practice, you'll find your confidence and intuition growing.

The Little Book of Spells contains spells that work for the good of all. When you learn to channel your natural powers, you'll be able to make changes in the natural world. The more open you are to these natural powers, the easier it will be to make magic.

Best of luck on this enchanting adventure!

S. S. Z.

WHAT IS A SPELL?

A spell is a will-driven mechanism that brings about a desired outcome. Simply put, a spell focuses positive energy to help you get what you want. Spell weavers employ symbols, words, and tools to achieve their goals. The energy generated by their rituals is directed out into the universe to generate change. Spells are not a substitute for conventional means of problem solving. They can work in tandem with mundane steps by providing an extra push to attract positive energy.

Many different types of spells exist. Most call upon archaic words, phrases, and tools that have evolved over time. Repetition is thought to render spells more powerful. Often the most effective spells are simple ones you concoct yourself.

Spellcraft is most productive when we have a full understanding of what we are doing and why we are doing it. It requires that we understand not only how a spell is spun, but also our true motives.

GETTING IN TUNE

There are five prerequisites to effective spellwork.

A strong desire or need. Whatever your aim, you must want to accomplish it badly.

Self-knowledge. Get in tune with your inner self. Know your principles, motives, and goals.

Faith in the result. Imagine in vivid color the changes to be made. Believe in the rightness of the outcome. Spells work only when you feel deserving of your goals.

Respect for the process. Keep your magic work to yourself. Discussing your spells dilutes their potency. Too many cooks spoil the brew!

Knowledge to cast the spell from beginning to end. Rely on this handbook!

RULES OF THE GAME

Be Good

One of the time-honored precepts of spellcraft is that you must never cast a spell that could potentially harm you or anyone else. That's why this book contains only positive, beneficial spells. Before acting, ask yourself, "How will I cause the least

harm?" This can mean avoiding harmful activities and substances, like cigarettes. It also means respecting the earth and the animals that live on it. And it means we must avoid actions likely to cause pain to others. Spellwork reminds us of the golden rule: treat others as you would like to be treated.

Your inner sense of right and wrong will guide you in casting spells. Spellcraft requires deep thought and sensitivity. Call upon your conscience to determine if a spell feels "right." If you have doubts, start anew.

What Goes Around Comes Around (Thrice!)

Nowhere is this expression more true than in the world of spells and magic! The precept known as The Law of Three states that whatever energy you put out—negative or positive—will come back to you threefold. This karma is spellcraft's system of feedback. It reminds us not to take the practice lightly.

PREPARING A SPACE

*I*n order to spin spells, you need a place of your own. Your special place will provide you with a focal point for spellcasting and a storage area for your tools. Your space can be anywhere that's convenient and quiet. Just set up a table and cover it with a cloth. Place on your special table symbols of the four

JOY

elements: a bowl of sand, sea salt, or some stones to symbolize Earth; candles or a wand to symbolize Fire; incense to symbolize Air; a glass and bowl filled with water to symbolize—you guessed it!—Water. Have fun decorating the table with herbs, flowers, stones, pentagrams, talismans, a spell box, and other magical tools.

love

MAGIC CIRCLES

*A*round your space imagine the presence of a magic circle. Historically, spell casters would enter a magic circle to unite in harmony with the forces of nature. The circle symbolizes the creation of the cosmos, the womb of Mother Earth, the idea of wholeness, and the seasons of life. Entering a magic circle is like entering a doorway into your soul. Inside, the possibilities for concentration and transcendence abound.

To banish negative energy from your circle, sweep the area with a broom, or purify it by sprinkling saltwater. Use your finger to trace a circle on the floor around your space or circle the area with cord. The circle may be opened and closed for exiting and entering at any time.

Magic Tools

Spellcraft makes use of various tools and props to enhance its effectiveness. Remember to always use natural fibers and tailor your tools and color choices to the spell you're casting.

CANDLES

Candles are a must for spell work. Besides representing Fire, they help focus the mind. In spellcraft, colors evoke different meanings, so choose the candle color with specific qualities in mind (see pages 20-21). Candles may be rubbed with essential oils or scored with special symbols that represent your

wish. They should be left to burn down completely. Those used for decoration should not be re-lit for use in magic spells.

STONES

It's hard to believe that inanimate stones and crystals

could be so alive with magical potential. These enchantingly beautiful objects symbolize our earthly nature, providing a link between the physical world and the magical realm (See Table, p. 75). Before use, stones should be cleansed with saltwater and energized by gentle tapping or exposure to the light of a full moon.

COLOR PROPERTIES

Red

Energy, passion, warmth, vitality, courage,
enthusiasm, creativity, strength, lust, willpower

Pink

Love, romance, tenderness, affection,
friendship, beauty, hope, harmony, optimism,
spiritual healing, compassion

Orange

Motivation, adaptability, encouragement, courage,
opportunity, friendship, success, enthusiasm

Yellow

Cheerfulness, joy, light, confidence, warmth,
communication, creativity, intelligence, charm

Green
Independence, growth, prosperity, healing, fertility, luck

Blue
Sincerity, calm, devotion, fidelity, healing, serenity,
truth, wisdom, pleasant dreams, protection

Purple
Ambition, power, prestige, spirituality, insight

White
Clarity, hope, protection, peace, purity, tranquility.
White can be substituted for any other color.

Black
Banishing, absorbing negative energy

Brown
Concentration, stability

peppermint

lemongrass

eucalyptus

st. john's wort

sandalwood

chamomile

OILS

Oils are essential! Their uses include healing, empowering, blessing, banishing, and anointing. They smell heavenly and are very potent (See Table, p. 74). They should be diluted with a carrier oil, such as vegetable or almond. When mixing oils, bear in mind how the scents will combine. For an added burst of energy, add herbs or crystals to your oils.

HERBS

From the earliest days of civilization, many major thinkers and writers have viewed nature as the ultimate reflection of divine truths. It's not surprising, therefore, that herbs possess unique characteristics, making them a mainstay in spellwork. Unlike other botanicals, herbs are extraordinarily hardy, requiring only a ray of sun, a few drops of water, and a little fresh air to thrive. Their hardiness carries over into spellwork, where they are distinguished by powerful magical properties (See Table, p. 78). Their scents are intoxicating, too!

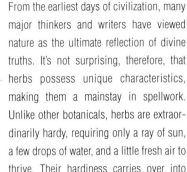

FOODS

Ever since the Garden of Eden, the world has known that foods possess magical properties. Some foods, such as apples, strawberries, and figs, are known to have aphrodisiacal charms. But the power of food transcends the world of love. Want to restore an old friendship? Try almonds. Thinking babies? Try rice, cucumbers, bananas, grapes. Need some extra spending money? Have a few cashews. Need a little lift? You guessed it—**chocolate!**

TREES AND LEAVES

Trees provide us with many gifts: shelter from the elements, wood for crafting, and oxygen for breathing. Their leaves, roots, bark, and flowers possess abundant magical properties with many different applications (See Table, p. 80).

FLOWERS

lowers constitute one of nature's most beautiful gifts. All over the world, flowers are given as tokens of love, appreciation, and comfort. They have a universal power to move us. It is this connection between nature and our emotions that

rose

daffodil

iris

26

makes flowers so magically potent (See Table, p. 79).

Simple spell:

Choose the bud of a flower that harmonizes with your
goal and place it in a vase filled with water. Write a spell
on a piece of paper next to it. When the bud blossoms,
the magic will be "fixed."

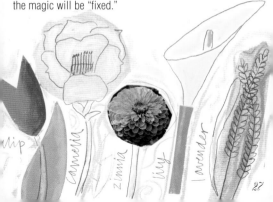

tulip

camelia

zinnia

ivy

lavender

PEN AND PAPER

Whether you choose a pen that's antique or new, quilled or of hand-blown glass, be sure to use it only for writing spells. You may also use a pencil. Ink or pigment colors should correspond to the spell you're casting. If you are writing a spell for healing, use blue. For energy, use red. You

should also have some paper—parchment or conventional—for use in spells that require writing, and a journal for recording your spells for future re-use.

SPELL BOX

A spell box is a kit that houses tools for a particular spell. Simply decorate the outside of a box with your favorite images, symbols, and colors. You may choose to line it with fabric. Inside the box, place stones, oils, and herbs that mirror your spell's intent. You might also include a symbol of your favorite hobby (e.g., a shoelace, if you're a runner), a drop or two of your favorite aromatherapy oil on a piece of cloth, a clipping of your hair, a photograph, and anything else that helps to personalize the spell.

To enhance the magic, place in the box a paper describing your wish in detail. Display the box on your magic table, surrounded by candles and flowers of the appropriate symbolic color. Say or chant your spell. Leave the written wish in the box until it comes true.

PENTAGRAM

he pentagram is a five-pointed star that can be used in spells to banish negative energy and to invoke positive energy. It can be placed on the magic table for protection. The points of the pentagram represent the four elements—Earth, Air, Water, Fire—and Spirit. The pentagram is often misconstrued as having evil or dark properties, but the reverse is actually true: it has been used through the ages as a powerful symbol of protection from harm.

The pentagram symbolizes practicality, stability, material wealth, and the earth. It is sometimes referred to as the "Endless Knot" because it can be drawn with a single line.

Magic Spells

*L*ong ago, people had little time for weaving elaborate spells, and they found enchantment in the rituals of daily life. The modern tendency to use complex procedures and trappings can hinder a positive outcome in spellcraft. Spell weavers who believe "less is more" find themselves freer to focus.

Spells are deeply personal. Feel free to modify spells according to what's available as well as what works best for you. This book gives many options and substitutions. You can always use white if you lack a certain color. If a spell is "most effective" on a Friday, but it's Tuesday, and you need to do it now—do so. The intensity of your feeling is a potent force that influences a spell's efficacy.

THE "NIGHT TO REMEMBER" SPELL

Supplies:

- A CD of your favorite love song
- Red pen or marker and slip of white paper
- Vanilla or jasmine incense

Light the incense and play the song. Write the first and last name of your date in lower case on the paper, leaving an extra space between each letter. In the open spaces, write your own name in upper case, so that the two names become one. *For example, Ben Smitten + Emma Star = EbMeMnA sSmTiAtRten.* Don't worry if the number of letters in the names is unequal. Place the paper in the CD case along with the CD. Open the box only to play the special song on the special date.

ATTRACTING
NEW LOVE

Simple, yet works every time!

Supplies:

- Pink or red candle
- Pink or red rose on stem
- Vanilla, jasmine, rose, or patchouli oil

Carefully cut a thorn off the rose. Tack the thorn into the center of the candle. Drizzle a few drops of oil on the candle. After burning the whole taper, you will attract a new love within 28 days, the cycle from new moon to new moon.

Other love ideas:

Make romance blossom by planting a "Love Window Box" with tulips, violets, asters, pansies, and poppies. Eat love-enhancing foods like apricots, apples, strawberries, tomatoes, cherries, and, last, but never least, chocolate!

lemon oil

KEEPING THE
FLAME ALIVE

Supplies:

- Favorite romantic novel
- An item of red clothing
- A piece of red ribbon
- Photograph of your boyfriend, preferably with you in it

Wear something red. Open the book to the most romantic passage. Place the photograph and ribbon on that page. With the book still open, chant: *On the wings of Cupid, With the luck of Fortuna, May time fan the flames of love.* Now close the book and chant: *Our love is so strong, It cannot be wrong, The magic is cast—So Be It.* As long as the book is kept in a safe place, with the picture and ribbon inside, your passion will smolder and withstand the test of time.

A BEAUTY SPELL
FOR CONFIDENCE

Supplies:

- A rose quartz crystal
- 8 rose petals
- A mirror
- Witch hazel poured into a clear glass jar or bottle
- Cotton balls or tissue

Using a mirror, take a close look at your face. Focus on the features and aspects that you find pretty and notice how they dominate your face, making it beautiful. Visualize the imperfections disappearing as you rub the rose quartz crystal over them. Then put the stone in the jar of witch hazel. Take the rose petals in your hands and let them lightly graze your face. Then place them in the jar/bottle. Cap it tightly and gently shake. Use this beauty tonic each day as an après-bath toner.

SPELL TO ENCOURAGE FRIENDSHIP

Supplies:

- A pink cloth or bandana
- A turquoise stone or jewelry with turquoise in it
- Two linked paper clips
- Rose petals or dried vanilla beans
- A small chime or whistle
- Rose or vanilla oil (optional)

To attract new friends and reconnect with old ones, prepare a charm as follows: Place the turquoise and paper clips on the pink cloth. Sprinkle with rose petals or dried vanilla beans. Sound the chime three times, repeating this incantation: *With this spell, I sound a chime, and bring friendship to this place in time*. If you have a whistle instead of a chime, modify the chant as follows: *With this spell, a whistle I blow, and watch my friendships bloom and grow.*

The potency of this spell may be enhanced by dabbing yourself in the morning with rose or vanilla oil. For a week, keep the interlocking paper clips close to your heart (a jacket pocket will do).

Enjoy the friendly, long-lasting effects of this spell.

"LONG LIVE OUR FRIENDSHIP" BRACELET

Supplies:

- Three lengths each of yellow yarn, string, embroidery floss or lanyard in yellow, in your favorite color, and in your friend's favorite color

- A small charm, bead, or symbol of something you've enjoyed together (e.g., a small seashell, if you've enjoyed the beach together)

To determine the proper length, wrap the lengths of string around your wrist twice, then add an extra nine inches. Knot all nine lengths of string together, incorporating the charm into the knotted end. (If you're using a seashell or other similar object, it must have a hole so that string can be run through it.) Leave enough of a tail at the end for closure—usually four or five inches. Use the three lengths of color as one strand and braid the lengths together. As you braid, repeat the following chant: *Friends forever, we are as one, Bound together in joy and fun.* Knot the ends together and tie around your wrist. This spell will work within fourteen days if the friendship is meant to be.

SPELL TO HELP A
FRIEND IN NEED

Supplies:

- White, blue, or pink tissue, rice paper or parchment
- Water-soluble pen or marker in orange or green
- Bowl of water

The most important thing to remember about this spell is that you must first ask your friend for permission to cast it, so you won't violate his or her privacy. Once cast, this spell is supremely effective.

Write your wish on a small slip of paper. Place the paper in the bowl of water and let the ink dissolve. Ask your friend to wash her hands in the water. She can also dab herself with the water, or it can be sprinkled over a path where she is likely to walk.

SPELL TO GAIN FORGIVENESS

Supplies:

- Shoebox top filled with sand or dirt. Or, if you are outside, just work in the soil.
- Wooden stick
- Quart-size bottle of naturally sparkling water

Using the stick, write a word in the sand symbolizing your offense. Pour the water over the word to erase it. Continue pouring until the offense has been symbolically washed away. Reflect on the offense and vow to try not to repeat it. Then say: *With this water I now end/The pain I sadly caused my friend. Sparkling water, cleanse my soul/With forgiveness make me whole.*

KNOT SPELL FOR PEACE

*T*he tying and untying of knots carries its own brand of magic in many folk spells. The process works to bind and release energy. In this spell, use white string or cord, symbolizing peace. Tie nine knots and chant while visualizing the objective of peace. By the ninth knot, the spell is fixed and the magic power stored within the knots.

With knot one, my spell's begun,
May its power soar; it's for everyone.
With knot two, pure as mountain dew,
My motive is that this wish come true.
With knot three, find harmony,
From ocean floor to the tallest tree.
By knot of four, open the door:

End suffering and banish war.
With knot five, for peace we'll strive.
In tying this cord, my goal comes alive.
With knot six, to wings adhere,
My wish for peace, an end to fear.
When seven knots adorn my cord,
Be there peace at home and peace abroad.
In tying knot eight,
Let peace be our fate.
And with knot nine
Peace and love intertwine.

To undo string magic, say this:
With each knot that I undo,
Free the magic, let it spew.
By my spell no one's been hurt,
It is my will that it revert.

*R*emember: Protection spells can be wonderfully effective, but they do not give us license to act irresponsibly or carelessly. Even the most potent protection spell is not foolproof. Enjoy the benefits of protection spells, but please remember what your mother told you: keep your seat belt fastened, don't take candy from strangers, and drive carefully!

SAFETY SACHETS & CHARM BAGS

Sachets and charm bags can be filled with a variety of magical ingredients effective in working many kinds of magic. With their potent properties, they prove that great things do come in small packages.

Supplies:

- Two square pieces of fabric in white or blue, or in predominantly white or blue accents
- Needle and white or blue thread—or—
- White, blue, or natural ribbon, satin cording, raffia
- A pinch of three of these herbal ingredients: vervain, angelica, St. John's wort, mistletoe, nettle, slippery elm, or, use common herbs: cloves, parsley, cinnamon, rosemary, chamomile, bay leaves, sage.
- Decoration: fabric paint, glue, sequins, beads, appliqués, buttons; small pieces of amethyst, garnet, turquoise, or lapis lazuli (optional)
- Glue

For the sewn sachet, align two pieces of fabric, right side to right side. Sew together three sides, leaving only one unsewn. Turn the material inside out to conceal the seams.

Decorate the sachet with the objects listed above, which will symbolize your wish for protection. Remember that the colors blue and white hold special protective properties. Once the glue is dry, fill the pouch with the herbal ingredients, leaving room to close the final open edge. With a looping overhand stitch, sew the open edge closed.

For the bundled sachet, use one piece of fabric at least five inches square. Lay the square flat, right side down, and place the herbal contents in the center. Bundle it up and use cording or ribbon to tie it off. Trim excess fabric off the top. Pinking shears give a nice scalloped or jagged edge. Glue symbolic decorations to the ends of the cording, to enhance the sachet's protective power.

"DON'T MESS WITH ME" FOLK CHARMS

To protect yourself, wear or carry coral, amethyst, diamond, pearl, ruby, carnelian, peridot, turquoise or sapphire, a tortoise shell bracelet, a necklace of rowan (mountain ash) berries, oak or rowan leaves.

For safe travel place a sprig of mint in your wallet, handbag, luggage, or glove compartment. Wear white clothing and turquoise and moonstone jewelry. Oh, and don't forget—55 is a lucky travel number.

To protect your space, place pine needles on the floor; twigs of papaya over the door; rosemary in the corners of a room; a pair of open scissors over the front door to cut off negativity from the outside. Place lavender near your pillow to bring sweet dreams; a full glass of water by your bed each night to collect negativity from the room; a cluster of acorns on the front door; St. John's Wort over doorways on a midsummer's eve; plum branches over doors and windows.

If you're in a park or walking down a tree-lined street, try standing under an oak tree or knocking on a willow tree.

Use your imagination to deflect negative energy. Envision your body as being shielded by a magic circle of pure white light; mirrors that face outward, away from you; a force field; a dense hedge; angel wings.

S.O.S! Did you know that the Titanic might never have sunk if only its passengers had known to wear or carry hazel sprigs or moonstones? Both the herb and the stone have magic properties that protect against shipwreck!

SPELL TO BE MORE FORGIVING OF OTHERS

Supplies:

- Several sprigs of mint
- Small length of white ribbon
- A small amount of saltwater in a white dish

Tie the mint stems with white ribbon. Dip the leaves into the purifying saltwater, and say: *I wash away judgment and scorn. Tolerance and patience in me be born. All disdain I hereby clear; Let forgiveness now be near.* **Remain on "inner grouch" alert and renew this spell whenever necessary!**

BATH TO WARD OFF
NEGATIVE ENERGY

Supplies:

- 1 pinch dried sage
- 1 pinch dried thyme
- 1/2 teaspoon dried basil
- 2 bay leaves
- Small square of cheesecloth or other material
- Small piece of string

This bath will fortify you against hostility from others for 24 hours. Place the ingredients in the pouch cloth and tie it off with string, and place in a bathtub filled with temperate water. Immerse yourself in the bath for ten minutes. Focus on affirming your inner strength and empowering yourself to withstand negativity that may come your way.

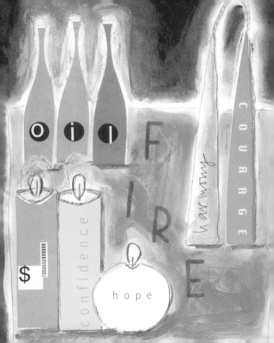

MAGIC OIL PROTECTION SPELL

Supplies:

- 1/4 cup of almond, jojoba, or vegetable oil as base
- 3 drops of lime oil
- 2 drops of patchouli oil
- 1 drop of yarrow oil, if available (or oil of black pepper, clove, pettigrain, cypress, juniper, or palmarosa)

Combine ingredients. Charge the oil by imagining it as infused with your energy. Take 3 deep breaths. Chant as follows: *Protect and save me from all harm/Let these oils now work their charm.* Now, daub yourself with the oil. Draw a pentagram on your forehead using a tiny amount. Take care not to let the oil drip into your eyes. Take comfort in its magical protective powers.

SIZZLE SPELL TO PROTECT YOUR BELONGINGS

Supplies:
- A pencil, nail, or pointed wooden stick for carving
- A white candle
- The object you wish to protect, or a photo

Use the pointed tool to carve your name into the candle from top to bottom, so the candle will burn in concert with your wish. Light the candle and focus on the flame. Visualize its heat passing into the object you wish to protect. Once you see the object as white hot, hold your hands above it (or photo), and say: *Too hot to touch!* Allow the candle to burn completely. This spell is perfect for an object of sentimental value. It lasts for thirty days.

PROTECT YOUR SPACE WITH AN HERBAL BOUQUET

Supplies:

- Sprigs of dried rosemary, lavender or juniper
- A garlic bulb (optional)
- Lilies on their stems (optional)
- A length of white ribbon, thread, or cord

Herbal bouquets can be hung upside down in the kitchen or above a door, protecting your home from harm. Tie the herbs and/or lilies in a bouquet using the white cord. Hang the bouquet to keep your home safe and sound.

lemon

SPELLS TO SUPPRESS GOSSIP AND WARD OFF JEALOUSY

Anti-Gossip Supplies:

- An item of your own clothing
- Lemon water: cold water with lemon rind in it

To suppress gossip, perform this ritual which will effectively return it to the sender. Take an item of your own clothing, a shirt for example, and turn it inside out. Place it in a doorjamb or on a windowsill and slam the door or window on it. The magic is effective immediately. Open or lift the door or window and turn the clothing right side out. Close the door or window and put the shirt back in its place. For further insurance against gossip, sprinkle lemon water on the path of the offender(s).

Anti-Envy Supplies:

- Cinnamon
- Cornstarch (or unscented talcum powder)

To protect yourself against the envy of others, take a pinch of cinnamon and dab it on your breastbone while you are dressing. Or, mix the cinnamon with cornstarch and use it as an after-bath dusting powder. Cinnamon is a very powerful protective spice that will benefit you immeasurably.

OAK

ROWAN

HAZEL

apple

"TURN OVER A NEW LEAF" SPELL

Supplies:

- A large green leaf
- A stick of cinnamon or allspice incense

With your finger, trace the word "success" on the leaf's surface. Bring the leaf and incense outdoors. Make sure the breeze catches the smoke as you light the incense. Now let fly the leaf toward the north. No matter how long it flutters before falling to the ground, **your wish for prosperity will take flight.**

Hint: If incense is unavailable, toss a handful of rice in the air before you let your leaf go. Rice has great magical properties associated with abundance and bounty.

"NO MORE FEARS"
SPELL

Hint: The first step in overcoming fear is to determine where it's coming from. Wear or carry an aquamarine or leopard skin jasper. The crystal's energies will give you the courage to locate the source of your fear.

Supplies:

- Orange or red pen or pencil
- White paper
- A pinch of ground ginger or thyme

List your fears on paper using orange or red ink. Shred the paper. Place the ripped-up pieces in a fireproof saucer. Sprinkle the ginger or thyme on top, and light. Wash the ashes down the drain, along with your fears.

ANGER COOL-DOWN BATH

Supplies:

- Incense of basil, lemon balm, lavender and/or thyme, or your favorite scent
- A blue candle
- Eucalyptus oil, or your favorite oil

Fill the tub with warm water. Rub the candle with the oil. Light both the candle and the incense. Inhale deeply and step into the tub. Lie down and immerse yourself four times; picture the water washing your anger away. After the bath, focus on the water swirling down the drain, carrying with it your last angry feelings.

"LAND THAT JOB"
SPELL

Supplies:

- 3 bay leaves—highly effective for granting wishes!
- An advertisement, logo, or other paper symbol of the job that you want

To make your dream job become a reality, fold the symbolic paper into thirds. Concentrate on your wish, imagining yourself in your ideal working environment. Place three bay leaves anywhere inside the folds of the paper. Fold the paper into thirds once more. Place the paper somewhere safe—in a spell box, for example. Once your wish is granted and the dream job is yours, carefully burn the magic paper as a gesture of thanks.

CHARM FOR GOOD HUMOR

When times are tough it's not easy to see the humor in things, but once you can laugh again, you'll never doubt the healing properties of a good sense of humor.

Supplies:

- An amusing photo of yourself
- A simple wooden frame
- Glue
- Feathers—for fun!
- Agate crystals—for smiles!
- A few small trinkets/charms that represent things you love to do
- A few drops of almond oil—to smooth the wrinkles

Place the photo in the frame and decorate it with the above items. As you affix each one, remind yourself of what it symbolizes. Then think about the three funniest things you can 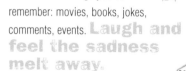 remember: movies, books, jokes, comments, events. Laugh and feel the sadness melt away.

Hint: A variation on the photo charm is to collect symbolic items and place them in a small bag or pouch to make a good humor charm bag. Carry it with you as a reminder to lighten up and laugh a little.

THE HAPPINESS POMANDER

This enchanting decoration will make you feel good whenever you're near it.

Supplies:

- An orange (or a lemon, lime, or grapefruit)
- Cloves (or allspice beads)
- A toothpick
- Ribbon—yellow, orange, or other happy color
- Sandalwood or sweetpea oil, or whatever essential oil you love

Poke holes in the orange to form a picture that illustrates your goal of feeling happy. Consider a smiley face, a heart, or whatever floats your boat. Push the cloves into the holes. Dab the fruit with a few drops of essential oil. Secure a ribbon around it. Hang it in an area where you can enjoy the splendor of its fragrant magic!

lemon

LIFE IS GOOD!

Hint: Try hanging the pomander in your closet or near a window so that its scented energy will fill the air. And don't worry that your pomander appears to be shrinking before your eyes. The orange base will shrink over time, but its magical fruity powers will last. When the scent fades, just dab the orange with a little more oil.

my favorite oil

SPELL TO MEND A BROKEN HEART

Supplies:

- Chamomile tea
- Honey
- Lemon wedge
- White cloth napkin

This spell works best on a Friday. Prepare a cup of chamomile tea near an open window. Add two teaspoons of honey to sweeten your experience. Add the juice of the lemon. Place the cup on the white napkin. Take one small sip and repeat these words three times: *As I sip this chamomile, Help me find a way to heal.* Now sip twice and repeat three times: *Joy now come and pain is through, As I commence to drink this brew!* Notice the gradual but certain emergence of a happier, brighter outlook.

STRAWBERRY FIELDS HEARTBREAK RELIEF SPELL

Supplies:

- One whole, plump strawberry
- A small paring knife

Appreciate the common characteristics of a strawberry and a heart: the rich redness, the form, the vibrancy. Remove greens and hull. Cut the strawberry in half to symbolize a broken heart. Hold the halves together. Place the whole fruit in your mouth, imagining your heart whole again. As you savor its nectar, repeat these

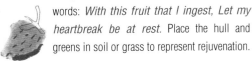

words: *With this fruit that I ingest, Let my heartbreak be at rest.* Place the hull and greens in soil or grass to represent rejuvenation.

SPELL TO HELP HEAL THE EARTH

Supplies:

- Seven freshly plucked petals or leaves
- A map or photo of the endangered area (optional)

On a sunny morning bring the petals or leaves to a needy area—urban, suburban, rural. Ascribe a day of the week to each petal or leaf. Facing north—the direction associated with earthly abundance—release the petals one by one, starting with Sunday. Chant: *Let fall these petals in a gentle breeze/With healing powers from the trees./On their surface rests my spell:/That this Earth be strong and well.* If the area you wish to restore is inaccessible, release the petals or leaves onto a photograph or map of the area.

Oils

Oil	Magical Properties
Basil	Harmony, peace, sympathy, happiness, love, prosperity
Chamomile	Dreams, calming anger, peace, meditation
Cinnamon	Energy, lust, prosperity, abundance
Eucalyptus	Health, purification, healing, protection
Lemon Balm	Love, healing, soothing heartbreak and depression, calming anger
Lemongrass	Psychic ability, friendship
Patchouli	Energy, attraction, sexual vitality
Peppermint	Health, healing, love, sleep, psychic ability, mental energy, overcoming shock
Rose	Beauty, calming anger, love, luck, protection, psychic ability, friendship, faithfulness
Sage	Wisdom, longevity, luck
St. John's Wort	Strength, managing stress, protection
Sandalwood	Sex, healing, spirituality, protection, mental powers, confidence
Vanilla	Friendship, love, wishes, prosperity, mental awareness

Stones

Stone	Associations
Agate	Depression relief, strength, business success
Amethyst	Psychic energy, happiness, love, stress management
Aquamarine	Courage, peace, balance, emotional cleansing
Garnet	Compassion, friendship, strength and energy, protection
Jade	Longevity, wisdom, prosperity, fertility, peace, luck, love
Jasper	Energy, beauty, health, protection, relief from nightmares
Lapis lazuli	Healing, fidelity, joy, love, beauty, business success
Moonstone	Harmony, travel, youth, sleep, emotional strength
Obsidian (black)	Stability, turning away negativity
Opal	Perceptiveness, beauty, emotional balance, creativity
Pearl	Calming of anger, luck
Rose quartz	Happiness, love, emotional healing, beauty, friendship
Sapphire	Inspiration, meditation, peace, power, prosperity
Tiger's Eye	Common sense, honesty, depression relief, energy
Turquoise	Friendship, luck, protection from negative acts, healing

aquamarine

garnet

opal

Foods

Food	Associations
Almonds	Friendship, wisdom, money, moderation, happiness
Apples	Love, romance, healing, fitness
Avocados	Lust, love, physical beauty
Bananas	Prosperity, potency, fertility, valor
Barley	Love, protection, celebration, discomfort reduction
Blackberries	Healing, prosperity, success
Celery	Psychic/mental abilities
Chocolate	Love, lifts spirits
Corn	Protection, luck
Figs	Love
Grapes	Mental and visual perceptiveness, fertility
Lemons	Mental clarity, purification, commitment, longevity
Oranges	Luck, health, love, fidelity
Pineapple	Love, prosperity, protection, healing, friendship
Rice	Fertility, prosperity, abundant blessings
Strawberries	Love, luck, intensity, romance, zest
Vanilla	Attracts men, mental awareness

apple

lemon

strawberries

BANANAS

Herbs

Herb	Associations
Allspice	Luck, lust, prosperity, health/healing
Angelica	Joy, promotes a feeling of welcome
Bay Leaf	Love, protection from illness, removal of negativity
Chamomile	Sleep, love, peace, protection
Cinnamon	Lust, success, energy, prosperity, protection
Cloves	Lust, love, depression/grief relief, luck
Garlic	Protection, good health
Lavender	Healing, longevity, sleep, childbirth
Mint	Success, refreshment
Nutmeg	Love, money, commitment, luck, healing, fidelity
Parsley	Lust, purification, protection (especially from accidents)
Sage	Wisdom, longevity, prosperity
Rosemary	Youthful energy, remembrance, protection
St. John's Wort	Protection, strength, stress management
Thyme	Romance, rest, health, courage
Vervain	Protection, sound sleep, wishes

Flowers

Flower	Associations
Buttercup	Pleasure, love, youthful energy, prosperity, happiness
Camellia	Gratitude, wealth
Daffodil	Love, good fortune
Daisy	New beginnings, simplicity
Honeysuckle	Prosperity, joy, psychic awareness
Iris	Stress relief, courage, wisdom
Jasmine	Confidence, self love
Lavender	Joy, peace, sleep, purification
Lilac	Beauty, love, protection
Lily	Protection, strength, purity
Pansy	Contemplation
Rose	Love, luck, new beginnings
Sunflower	Wisdom, fertility, health, creativity
Sweetpea	Friendship, truth
Tulip	Joy, love, dreams
Violet	Gentleness, quiet
Zinnia	Passion, strength, love

Trees

Tree/Leaf	Associations
Apple	Love and romance
Ash	World unity, health, motherhood
Birch	New beginnings
Dogwood	Protects secrets
Elm	Communication
Grapevine	Joy, festivity, celebration, happiness
Hawthorn	Help break bad habits, rid oneself of negative energy
Hazel	Knowledge, perceptiveness
Oak	Protection from harm, luck, prosperity
Pine	Banishing negativity, protection, fertility, prosperity, zest, vigor, health, longevity
Rowan (Mountain Ash)	Creativity, health, physical energy, vibrancy
Willow	Love, protection, healing, easing the end of a phase or relationship, new beginnings, adaptability